Pupil Book 3

Vocabulary, Grammar and Punctuation

Author: Abigail Steel

William Collins' dream of knowledge for all began with the publication of his first book in 1819. A self-educated mill worker, he not only enriched millions of lives, but also founded a flourishing publishing house. Today, staying true to this spirit, Collins books are packed with inspiration, innovation and practical expertise. They place you at the centre of a world of possibility and give you exactly what you need to explore it.

Collins. Freedom to teach.

Published by Collins
An imprint of HarperCollins*Publishers*
The News Building
1 London Bridge Street
London
SE1 9GF

Browse the complete Collins catalogue at
www.collins.co.uk

British Library Cataloguing in Publication Data
A Catalogue record for this publication is available from the British Library

Edited by Hannah Hirst-Dunton
Cover design and artwork by Amparo Barrera
Internal design concept by Amparo Barrera
Typesetting by Jouve India Private Ltd
Illustrations by Beatriz Castro, Aptara and QBS

Printed in Italy by Grafica Veneta S.p.A.

Contents

Using a dictionary

You can use a **dictionary** to find the meanings of words and to check their spellings. The words in dictionaries are in **alphabetical order**.

- For the word **bed**:

  bed noun

  a piece of furniture used for sleeping

  (plural **beds**)

Get started

Put these words into alphabetical order. One has been done for you.

1. milk, bread, eggs, cheese

   Answer: *bread, cheese, eggs, milk*

2. lion, tiger, elephant, giraffe

3. apples, oranges, bananas, grapes

4. jump, run, dance, spin

5. book, tablet, newspaper, magazine

6. cow, sheep, dog, horse

7. netball, hockey, cricket, rugby

8. pencil, ruler, eraser, notebook

Try these

Put these words into alphabetical order. One has been done for you.

1. clown, cracked, careful, comedy

  Answer: *careful, clown, comedy, cracked*

2. break, ball, bounce, bone

3. gnome, gate, great, garden

4. jewel, jam, jump, judge

5. pretty, perhaps, proper, photograph

6. heavy, heart, home, happy

7. trunk, terror, terrified, tackle

8. sofa, soda, tap, soap

Now try these

Read the sentences and look up the underlined words in a dictionary. Then follow the instruction in each sentence.

1. Draw a <u>feline</u>.

2. Draw a <u>jubilant</u> face.

3. Draw an <u>oblong</u>.

4. Draw something you could find in a <u>menagerie</u>.

5. Write what is <u>contrary</u> to **good**.

6. Write three words that show the use of <u>alliteration</u>.

Guide words

In a dictionary there are usually two **guide words** at the top of each page. They tell you the first word and the last word on that page. They help you to find words more quickly and easily, because all of the words on each page are the guide words themselves or come between the two guide words **alphabetically**.

- The word **accident** comes between the guide words **absorb** and **accordion**.

- The word **no** comes between the guide words **night** and **nutrition**.

- The word **related** comes between the guide words **rare** and **repair**.

Get started

Match each word to the guide words that would be at the top of its dictionary page. One has been done for you.

1. cash	**a)** pour – prance
2. mermaid	**b)** eject – elf
3. anchor	**c)** mention – mess
4. elephant	**d)** developing – different
5. protect	**e)** cart – castaway
6. powder	**f)** chip – clean
7. diagonal	**g)** amusement – anger
8. clamp	**h)** propel – protect

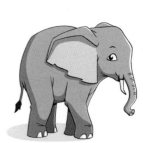

Try these

Write out three words that could be on a dictionary page showing these guide words. Give the words in alphabetical order. One has been done for you.

1. game – grow

   get, ghastly, grab

2. ham – huge

3. map – mug

4. paper – practice

5. sit – strain

6. take – toad

7. electric – eye

8. alternative – author

Now try these

Look up each word in a dictionary and write down the guide words on its page.

1. train

2. rabbit

3. sew

4. politics

5. baffle

6. hotel

Root words

A **root word** is a word that has a meaning **on its own**, without a prefix or a suffix. Prefixes and suffixes can be added to a root word, to change its meaning in some way. Root words cannot be broken down into any smaller words.

- **un-** (prefix) + **kind** (root word) = **unkind**

- **kind** (root word) + **-ness** (suffix) = **kindness**

- **un-** (prefix) + **kind** (root word) + **-ness** (suffix) = **unkindness**

Get started

Look at each list of words. Identify and write the one that is a root word. One has been done for you.

1. paying, uncover, think, gardener

   Answer: *think*

2. gladness, catch, misbehave, overcook

3. read, rerun, joyful, runner

4. undone, defenceless, old, danced

5. disallow, unfair, fullness, honey

6. farming, misunderstand, place, eaten

7. playful, man, underground, promised

8. fast, spends, cows, crossing

Try these

Copy out each list of words. Underline the root word that is inside each word and then write a sentence saying that it is the root word. One has been done for you.

1. <u>friend</u>ship, <u>friend</u>ly, un<u>friend</u>ly:

    Answer: *The root word is friend.*

2. kindness, unkind, kindest:

3. likelihood, likely, dislike:

4. playful, underplayed, playground:

5. rethink, thinking, thinker:

6. mistake, takeaway, taken:

7. working, workshop, housework:

8. builder, building, rebuild:

Now try these

Look at each word. Write down the root word that is inside it.

1. unwrap

2. careless

3. mishears

4. defrosted

5. repainting

6. uninterested

Nouns with prefixes

A **prefix** is a group of letters that can be added to the beginning of a word to change its meaning. There are lots of prefixes you can add to nouns to create new nouns.

Get started

Match each prefix to its meaning, using a dictionary to help you. One has been done for you.

1. *mis-*
2. dis- / in-
3. re-
4. inter-
5. sub-
6. super- / over-
7. anti-
8. auto-

a) again / back
b) against
c) not / lack of
d) bigger / more than usual
e) between
f) self / on its own
g) *bad / incorrect*
h) under / below

Try these

Copy out these sentences and underline the prefixes. One has been done for you.

1. I read a great <u>auto</u>biography.
2. Iron Man is a cool superhero.
3. We put antifreeze in the car when it was cold.
4. I use subheadings in my work.
5. Mum stared at the mess in disbelief.
6. It was just a misunderstanding.

Now try these

Copy and complete these sentences, adding a prefix from the box. Use a dictionary for help if you need to.

re-	dis-	de-	un-	mis-	in-

1. I wanted to watch the goal again, so I enjoyed the action ____play.
2. Jacqui thought that she had closed the window, but she had some ____certainty about it.
3. Mr Soames was frustrated by his ____ability to remember where his glasses were.
4. Dr Sengupta was sick of Beryl's ____behaviour.
5. Anthony put the bucket back in the garage having ____iced the pond.
6. I heard a loud ____agreement between my brothers.

Word families

Words can be grouped into **word families** based on their **root words**. This shows that they are related in some way – often by both spelling and meaning. However, root words are sometimes altered in spelling when they are used inside words in their word families.

- Root word **energy**: **energetic, energised, re-enervate**

Get started

Match each word to another from the same word family. One has been done for you.

1. *happiness*
2. actor
3. preparation
4. suspect
5. family
6. spectacles
7. speaker
8. horror

a) unprepared
b) familiar
c) horrifying
d) *unhappy*
e) reaction
f) suspicion
g) inspector
h) outspoken

Try these

Read the words that are in each word family and then write down the root word that joins them. Remember, root words are sometimes altered in spelling when they are used inside words in their word families. One has been done for you.

1. friendliness, unfriendly, befriend: *friend*

2. signature, signal, design:

3. standing, understood, grandstand:

4. giver, forgive, given:

5. possibility, impossible, impossibility:

6. singer, song, sung:

Now try these

Copy and complete each sentence, choosing one of the related words from the box.

1. We were helping the younger children to learn their _____.

2. The captain had to make a _____ about which direction to sail.

3. I have my school report, and I'm not sure how Mum will _____.

4. I could see the _____ building up in our teacher's eyes!

5. Kaseem had to _____ his spelling test.

telephone / phonics
decide / decision
react / actor
angrily / anger
repeat / repetition

Parts of a sentence (verbs)

A **verb** is a word that describes actions or feelings. A verb tells us what someone is doing or what is happening.

- Sam **sings**.

- Padma and Arthur **played** with the ball.

Get started

Copy out these sentences, underlining the verb in each one. One has been done for you.

1. The phone _rang_ at 7 a.m.

2. Mum and Aunty Diane were on the phone for more than half an hour.

3. Next Mum boiled the kettle, ready for her morning drink.

4. We go to school as quickly as possible.

5. Mum tunes the radio to a music station.

6. We all sing along with the song.

7. Surprisingly, we arrive at school on time.

8. My teacher will tick us off on the register in class.

Try these

Copy and complete these sentences by adding a suitable verb.
One has been done for you.

1. On Tuesday we _walked_ around the museum.

2. Samir _____ cricket.

3. The author _____ a story.

4. Finally, my parcel _____ in the post.

5. That kestrel is _____ low in the sky.

6. We will _____ with our dogs in the forest.

7. After school, Jamira _____ her flute.

8. Zoe _____ lots of fish at the aquarium.

Now try these

Copy and complete these sentences, using the verb forms in the box.

is	were	was	am	being	are

1. I _____ currently running through the park.

2. When I saw her, Victoria _____ giving Claus his birthday present.

3. It's ten o'clock, and we _____ all still waiting for Mr Cooke to arrive.

4. That _____ the biggest cake I've ever seen!

5. Yesterday, _____ Anton and Emilie at school with you?

6. Mario was _____ silly with the flour in our cookery lesson.

Parts of a sentence (nouns and adjectives)

Nouns name people, places, things and ideas.
Adjectives are words that tell us more about nouns.

- Nouns: **cow**, **field**, **gate**

- Adjectives: **enormous**, **excited**, **white**

Get started

Copy out each sentence, underlining the noun once and underlining the adjective twice. One has been done for you.

1. My <u>loud</u> <u>alarm</u> goes off and I get up.

2. I put on my blue uniform.

3. I go downstairs to eat my breakfast, which is tasty.

4. After that I brush my teeth until they are clean.

5. I comb my dark hair.

6. Then my striped tie goes on.

7. I pull on my coat, which is cosy.

8. Finally, I'm ready to leave for school!

Try these

Copy and complete these sentences by adding suitable nouns.
One has been done for you.

1. The _rain_ fell from the clouds and soaked us.
2. We went to the park for lunch and sat on a wooden _____.
3. I pulled my woolly _____ onto my hands to keep them warm.
4. Near the school gates is a busy _____, so we have to be careful.
5. Our cat likes to climb the _____, but sometimes he can't get back down!
6. The elegant _____ span and twirled across the stage.
7. We all gathered together so gran could take a family _____.
8. It had been a long _____, but now it was time to go _____.

Now try these

Copy and complete these sentences by adding suitable adjectives.

1. On the way to school we walk past a _____ building.
2. The wildlife park is full of _____ animals.
3. The _____ fireman climbed the tree easily.
4. We walked carefully over the _____ bridge.
5. When I get into school I hang up my _____ coat.
6. Gem's _____ little brother kicked the _____ leaves.

Pronouns to avoid repetition (1)

Pronouns can take the place of nouns. These can be proper nouns, like names.

- Pronouns: **I**, **me**, **you**, **he**, **him**, **she**, **her**, **it**, **we**, **us**, **they**, **them**

We use pronouns to stop us from repeating a noun.

- Sam knew **Sam** was different.
- Sam knew **he** was different.

Get started

Copy out these sentences, underlining the pronouns. One has been done for you.

1. Felix's mum gave <u>him</u> some jobs to do.
2. He was feeling grumpy.
3. Mum asked us to help.
4. She handed over a duster.
5. Mum gave me a sponge.
6. Felix took it and started to clean.
7. I took the duster instead.
8. Should we ask you to help, too?

Try these

Copy and complete these sentences by adding suitable pronouns. One has been done for you.

1. After Felix and I had dusted, mum said <u>we</u> should mop.

2. Mum said _____ would get out the mop and bucket.

3. The bucket was heavy, so _____ helped.

4. Mum sorted the bookcase and moved _____ to the next room.

5. I packed some old things into a box that Mum gave to _____.

6. The house looked great: _____ both thought that Dad would be pleased with _____ for helping.

Now try these

Copy and complete these sentences by replacing the underlined words with suitable pronouns.

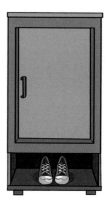

1. Ella's mum asked Ella to pick up the shoes in the hall. <u>Ella</u> put the shoes away in the tall cupboard.

2. Gita carried <u>Gita's</u> bag to the door and hung the bag up.

3. Tim's granddad asked Tim and Frances to tea. <u>Tim and Frances</u> were looking forward to seeing <u>Tim's granddad</u>.

4. Rani and I were starving – <u>Rani and I</u> ate everything that was given to <u>Rani and me</u>.

Pronouns to avoid repetition (2)

Possessive pronouns can take the place of possessive nouns.

- Possessive pronouns: my, mine, your, yours, his, her, hers, its, our, ours, their, theirs

Pronouns stop us repeating nouns.

- Non picked up **Non's** hat and pulled down **the hat's** brim.

- Non picked up **her** hat and pulled down **its** brim.

Get started

Copy out these sentences, underlining the possessive pronouns. One has been done for you.

1. Art is a skill for  sister Anya.

2. Anya entered a competition in her magazine.

3. Anya painted a picture of a flower growing in our garden.

4. Dad provided his best paints.

5. The colours were bright and their effect was beautiful.

6. When dry, the painting went into its envelope.

7. Now the judges would choose their favourite entry.

8. Finally, a letter for Anya came: the painting that had won the competition was hers!

Try these

Copy and complete these sentences by adding suitable possessive pronouns. One has been done for you.

1. My sister Anya and <u>our</u> mum ate lunch.

2. Afterwards, Anya went to see _____ friend.

3. They played with _____ shared toys.

4. Anya's friend Cam chose _____ favourite.

5. "That's _____ favourite, too!" said Anya.

6. Then Cam's dog ran in, chasing _____ tail.

7. Anya sees more of _____ friends than I see _____.

Now try these

Copy and complete these sentences by replacing the underlined words with suitable possessive pronouns.

1. Lots of children sent <u>the children's</u> competition entries in for <u>the competition's</u> prize draw.

2. Anya and <u>Anya's</u> family were proud – <u>Anya's and her family's</u> reaction was enthusiastic: "Let's celebrate!"

3. Dad said Anya and I could use <u>Dad's</u> garden tools because we enjoy growing <u>Anya's and my</u> flowers.

4. The dog tried to bury <u>the dog's</u> bone in the middle of <u>Anya's and my</u> flowerbed!

The present perfect tense

The present perfect tense tells us about something that has happened at some time in the past, when that time isn't made precise.

To make the present perfect form of verbs we add a helping verb, like **has** or **have**, to a **past participle**, like **left** or **eaten**.

- The owl **has** left the barn.

- I **have** eaten all the chocolate.

Get started

Copy out these sentences, underlining the helping verbs once and underlining the past participles twice. One has been done for you.

1. I <u>have</u><u>watched</u> the birds in my garden.

2. The black bird has eaten all of the sunflower seeds.

3. I have put more seeds out.

4. The robin has pecked our window.

5. I have wiped the window clean.

6. The neighbours' cat has seen the birds, too.

7. They have, so far, stopped him from chasing them.

8. He has still watched them closely.

Try these

Copy and complete these sentences by adding the correct helping verbs to the past participles. One has been done for you.

1. The eggs _have_ hatched.

2. The adult birds _____ gone to find food.

3. The cat _____ seen them flying around.

4. The cat _____ tried to climb the tree.

5. I _____ chased him away.

6. He _____ continued to prowl around.

7. The neighbours _____ put a bell on his collar.

8. The robin _____ learned to fly off when she hears it!

Now try these

Rewrite these sentences, changing the verbs into the present perfect form.

1. I ate my lunch.

2. Xavier finished his homework.

3. I went to York.

4. My brother saw the new film.

5. I looked after the fish.

6. I was asked to look after the school hamster.

Conjunctions (1)

A **conjunction** is a **joining word**.

- Conjunctions: **and**, **but**, **so**, **or**, **as**, **yet**, **if**, **because**

We can use a conjunction to join two sentences together to make one long sentence.

Get started

Copy out these sentences and underline the conjunctions. One has been done for you.

1. My gran moved house <u>and</u> I helped her.

2. She moved house because her old home was too big.

3. The new house is smaller but it is still lovely.

4. She moved in last Tuesday so I can visit any time.

5. She isn't settling into her new house, yet she likes her new neighbours.

6. She plays cards with them or they go walking.

7. She nearly lost her cat as she left him behind.

8. She would have been sad if the removal men had not found him.

Try these

Copy and complete these sentences by adding suitable conjunctions. One has been done for you.

1. The house needs to be dusted <u>*and*</u> it needs to be decorated.

2. Gran has settled in _____ now I can visit.

3. She lives further away from me now _____ she's close to Aunt Sue.

4. I'd love to spend time there _____ I like my aunt.

5. Perhaps I could go at weekends _____ I could stay for holidays instead.

6. I would stay ages _____ Aunt Cicely would have me.

7. I'm sad she's moved away _____ I'm excited about these plans.

Now try these

Join the sentences together using a suitable conjunction from the box.

| and | if | because | so | but | or |

1. Mum said I could visit Gran. I could finish my chores in time.

2. I have finished my chores for today. I can visit her tonight.

3. It takes an hour. I don't mind the journey.

4. I'm going to explore. I'm going to help Gran unpack.

5. She'll need help with the boxes. They are heavy.

Conjunctions (2)

There are lots of different conjunctions that have several different meanings.

- Some more conjunctions: **although**, **while**, **until**, **unless**, **after**, **when**, **before**, **since**

Sometimes conjunctions can be used at the **beginning** of a sentence, but not always.

- **Although** it rained, we went for a walk.

Get started

Copy out these sentences and underline the conjunctions. One has been done for you.

1. I did some chores at home <u>while</u> Dad took a nap.

2. I had to do my chores since I wanted to earn some pocket money.

3. I saved my money until I had £5.

4. Dad took me to town when he was free.

5. I wanted to look for some new art supplies since I don't have many.

6. I thought about buying a particularly stunning paint set although I couldn't afford it.

7. I decided I would come back for the paint set at the weekend unless I found something cheaper.

8. I looked around before I made my decision.

Try these

Copy and complete these sentences by adding suitable conjunctions. One has been done for you.

1. _Although_ I found some pens, they weren't the type I wanted.

2. I looked at the rulers _____ Dad looked at the books.

3. _____ I found the perfect set, I wouldn't buy any more paints.

4. I hadn't spotted any I liked _____ I'd seen the expensive sets.

5. Finally, I bought a pack of colouring pencils _____ I didn't have any.

6. We shopped _____ it was time to go home for tea.

7. _____ we got home we realised how tired we were!

Now try these

Use each of these conjunctions to join sentences of your own. Think carefully about what the different conjunctions mean.

1. because   2. although

3. while   4. until

5. if   6. before

Adverbs (1)

An **adverb** is a word that gives more meaning to a **verb** by adding details about how, when or where something happened. Many adverbs end in **-ly**.

- The sun shone **brightly**.
- Anwen ran **quickly**.

Get started

Copy out these sentences and underline the adverbs. One has been done for you.

1. Nia broke the glass <u>accidentally</u>.

2. Jon sings sweetly.

3. Sometimes I dance energetically.

4. Ms Quaver's dog barks tunefully.

5. Francine waves merrily and smiles.

6. It's important to live actively.

7. Theresa looked admiringly at Ana's top.

8. Nathan walked briskly to the shop.

Try these

Copy and complete each sentence by adding the most suitable adverb from the box. Look at where the adverb is placed and how it alters the meaning of the sentence. One has been done for you.

easily carefully angrily gently speedily happily directly slowly

1. I learn new languages _easily_.

2. Mrs Poppet shouts _____ at us.

3. The flowers sway _____ in the breeze.

4. We _____ ran to the playground, glad it was break time.

5. I ate my lunch _____ because I was hungry.

6. Move the delicate pot _____ so it doesn't break.

7. The snail glided _____ over the leaf.

8. Mum said we had to come home _____ after school.

Now try these

Rewrite these sentences, adding suitable adverbs that end in **-ly**.

1. We looked around the museum.

2. We were laughing.

3. It was raining.

4. Jolene ran for the bus.

5. Chuck opened his reading book.

6. The magpie flew towards the tree.

Adverbs (2)

An **adverb** is a word that gives more meaning to a **verb** or an **adjective** by adding details about how, when or where something happened.

Many adverbs end in **-ly**, but there are also lots that do not end in **-ly**: often, almost, well, very, ever, now, often, once, always, soon, yesterday, today, tomorrow, then, afterwards.

- Goldilocks ate breakfast and **then** went to sleep.

- The bears **always** go for a walk.

Get started

Copy out these sentences and underline the adverbs. One has been done for you.

1. Sandro went to a circus <u>yesterday</u>.

2. The circus is always fun.

3. Sandro got on well with his brother.

4. They had never been before.

5. They were very excited.

6. The performance is scheduled to start soon.

7. Things are different today.

8. The boys often argue about this.

Try these

Copy and complete each sentence by adding a suitable adverb from the box. Look at where the adverb is placed and how it alters the meaning of the sentence. One has been done for you.

| almost   ever   now   once   tomorrow   afterwards   first   next |

1. At the circus, the acrobats performed _first_.

2. The clowns rode into the ring _____.

3. Some dancers twirled around the edges _____.

4. The magicians showed their tricks and Sandro _____ guessed their secrets.

5. Sandro had _____ seen a magician at a party.

6. There are trained dogs performing _____, which everyone is enjoying.

7. Sandro thought it was the best day out he would _____ have.

8. It was a late night – he would have to sleep in _____.

Now try these

Rewrite these sentences, adding suitable adverbs that do not end in **-ly.**

1. We will eat fish and chips.

2. We visited the swimming baths.

3. Annika beat Isabella in the race.

4. Frankie enjoyed watching the sunset.

5. Henry was the best at writing stories.

6. You can come and visit me.

Prepositions of place

A **preposition** is a word that tells us how one thing is **connected** to another. Some prepositions tell the reader about locations or **places**.

- The cat sat **on** the mat.

- The twins are **at** school.

Get started

Copy out these sentences and underline the prepositions. One has been done for you.

1. Marcel is _at_ the airport.

2. His bags are on the conveyor belt.

3. Tony stood beside the check-in desk.

4. A baby crawled under the seat.

5. A luggage trolley rolled across the waiting room.

6. A jumbo jet soars above the city.

7. Erik's ticket was among his other papers.

8. Kelsie travelled down the escalator.

Try these

Copy and complete these sentences by adding suitable prepositions. One has been done for you.

| behind | inside | along | past | through | in | over | up |

1. The passengers queue up _behind_ one another.

2. They walk _____ the steps to the plane.

3. Everybody sits _____ the correct seat.

4. Hand luggage is placed _____ the overhead storage.

5. The cabin crew walk _____ the aisle.

6. An air steward walks _____ a crying baby, smiling at the mother.

7. He steps _____ the curtain into the kitchen area.

8. The plane is flying _____ the sea.

Now try these

Copy and extend these sentences by adding a preposition of place and some extra information.

For example: The plane is flying... _in the sky_.

1. The plane touches down smoothly…

2. The passengers leave the plane…

3. They collect their suitcases…

4. The suitcases were waiting for them…

5. Kelsie's family have booked a hotel…

6. George's father drives them to their house…

Prepositions of time

A **preposition** is a word that tells us how one thing is **connected** to another. Some prepositions tell the reader about the **time** an action happened.

- Tomas ate dinner **after** skateboarding.
- Nicola sharpened her pencil **before** the lesson.

Get started

Copy out these sentences and underline the prepositions. One has been done for you.

1. Dean helps his granny *during* the afternoons.
2. Oskar practised bowling before the cricket match.
3. Our train arrived as the clock struck two.
4. Fabienne has a guitar lesson on Thursdays.
5. Duane went for a run after lunch.
6. I couldn't stop reading until I reached the end!
7. The play starts at eight o'clock.
8. I have lunch around noon.

Try these

Copy and complete each sentence by adding the most suitable preposition of time from the box. One has been done for you.

for   during   after   at   on   since   following   throughout

1. Rafael has been waiting *for* three days.
2. Craig needed a large glass of water _____ training.
3. Tessa ate a biscuit _____ teatime.
4. Jasper tidied his room _____ playing.
5. Edward has a lie-in _____ Saturdays.
6. Jody has been dancing _____ she was six years old.
7. Nora's grandfather was asleep, and snored _____ the film!
8. Florence needed a drink _____ the night.

Now try these

Copy and extend these sentences by adding a preposition of time and some extra information.

For example: Charlie was nervous... *during her piano exam.*

1. Lucy wanted to giggle…
2. Samir has played the trumpet…
3. Xander went to meet his friends…
4. We went to see the film…
5. The bus arrived…
6. Rowena tried not to panic…

A or an?

We use **a** in front of a word that begins with a **consonant sound**. We use **an** before a word that begins with a **vowel sound**.

- **a c**at
- **an a**pple

Get started

Copy and complete these lists by adding **a** or **an**. One has been done for you.

1. *an* apple, *a* banana, *a* pear, *an* orange
2. __ pen, __ pencil, __ eraser, __ ruler
3. __ aeroplane, __ boat, __ train, __ car
4. __ police officer, __ doctor, __ artist, __ teacher
5. __ robin, __ sparrow, __ owl, __ blackbird
6. __ bee, __ ant, __ butterfly, __ wasp
7. __ actor, __ singer, __ dancer, __ author
8. __ second, __ minute, __ hour, __ day

Try these

Copy and complete these sentences by adding **a** or **an**. One has been done for you.

1. When I was tidying my room, I found _an_ old teddy bear and _a_ book.

2. Yannick had eaten __ packet of sweets and __ ice-cream.

3. For Kinaya's birthday we had __ pizza and __ enormous chocolate cake.

4. At the museum I saw __ interesting skeleton and __ huge old sword.

5. I made breakfast for my mum: toast, __ egg and __ bowl of cereal.

Now try these

Copy and complete the sentences below with a list of three items, using **a** or **an** before each item. Include at least one word that begins with a consonant sound and at least one word that begins with a vowel sound.

For example: In a zoo, I would find… _a lion, a tiger and an elephant._

1. In a supermarket, I would find…

2. On my face, I have…

3. At supper, I could have…

4. While birdwatching, I could see…

5. For school, I need…

Final punctuation

The first word of every sentence starts with a **capital letter**. There must also be some **final** punctuation at the end of a sentence.

We use a **full stop** (.) if the sentence is a statement. We use a **question mark** (?) if the sentence is a question. We use an **exclamation mark** (!) if a sentence would be said loudly or with lots of emotion – like surprise, anger or excitement.

- **A** fox walked through the forest**.**

- **W**here is the fox now**?**

- **T**he fox is chasing the horse**!**

Get started

Copy out each sentence and think about whether it is a statement, question or exclamation. Then label it 'correct' or 'incorrect' to show whether or not it has the correct punctuation. One has been done for you.

1. The fox has seen a rabbit!: *correct*

2. The rabbit looks startled?

3. Is the rabbit startled?

4. Where is the rabbit.

5. The rabbit hopped away.

6. Where has it gone!

7. The rabbit is hiding.

8. There it is!

Try these

Copy and complete these sentences by adding the correct punctuation and capital letters. Think about whether each sentence is a statement, question or exclamation. One has been done for you.

1. we were having fun in the forest

   Answer: *We were having fun in the forest.*

2. joey is stuck up a tree

3. can you reach her

4. i will try to climb up too

5. i am really scared

6. can you both get down

7. she climbed so high up

8. are you all right now

Now try these

For each topic, write one statement, one question and one exclamation. Make sure you use capital letters in the right places and punctuate the sentences correctly.

1. A picnic

2. Choosing an ice-cream

3. A trip to a forest

4. Going shopping

5. A lesson at school

6. Playing sport

Capital letters

Remember, every sentence starts with a **capital letter**. We also use capital letters at the beginning of **proper nouns**. Proper nouns are names or titles of things such as people, places, months, days, books and films.

- **M**y best friend is **M**artha.
- **S**he comes from **C**anada.
- **W**e have swimming every **M**onday.

Get started

Copy out the sentence from each pair that uses capital letters correctly. One has been done for you.

1. **a)** My birthday is in october.

   b) My birthday is in October.

   Answer: *b) My birthday is in October.*

2. **a)** my Cousin is a great Dancer.

   b) My cousin is a great dancer.

3. **a)** Fabien lives in paris in France.

   b) Fabien lives in Paris in France.

4. **a)** We have English on Thursdays.

   b) We have english on thursdays.

5. **a)** Elsa and I went to London.

   b) Elsa and i went to London.

6. **a)** My mum was born in a town in Florida.

   b) My mum was born in a Town in Florida.

Try these

Rewrite these sentences using capital letters in the correct places. One has been done for you.

1. newcastle is a city in england.

   Answer: *Newcastle is a city in England.*

2. newquay is a town in cornwall.

3. my friends are called naveen, tobias and elena.

4. my favourite days are tuesday and saturday, when i go swimming.

5. the film i enjoy most is *paddington*.

6. texas is a state in america.

7. my brothers are called phillip and john.

8. 'mr stink' is the book i enjoy reading most.

Now try these

Write your own sentence about each of these topics, making sure you use capital letters correctly.

1. A place you have visited

2. Your friends

3. TV programmes you like

4. When you have your birthday

5. Your favourite books

6. What you did at the weekend

Apostrophes for possession

We can use an **apostrophe** (') with the letter **s** to show **possession**. This is when something **belongs** to someone or something else.

- The **girl's** bike is blue.
- The **rabbit's** hutch is near the wall.

Get started

Copy out these sentences, underlining the words that use apostrophes to show possession. One has been done for you.

1. It's lucky the cat cannot reach the <u>*bird's*</u> nest.

2. Just outside the lion's den there's a large tree.

3. You wouldn't be able to steal from the dragon's lair.

4. She's not able to see the badger's set from the path.

5. It's as sticky as a spider's web!

6. Michael's dad has made sure there's cake for us.

7. I hadn't meant to take my friend's bag.

8. He's comes to collect it from my mum's house.

Try these

Copy and complete these sentences by adding apostrophes to show possession in the correct places. One has been done for you.

1. I borrowed my friends pencil.

   Answer: *I borrowed my friend's pencil.*

2. Staceys pencil snapped.

3. I used Miss Smiths sticky tape to fix it.

4. Sawyers kittens are so cute.

5. Jamies racing car whizzes past.

6. Santana used her sisters hairbrush without asking.

7. Sorrells bike crashed into Mrs Obermans fence.

8. Mr Checkett marked Deans and Brookes homework books.

Now try these

Rewrite each phrase using an apostrophe to show possession. Then put each phrase into a sentence of your own.

1. the spade belonging to the gardener

2. books belonging to Uncle Paul

3. the computer belonging to Millie

4. games belonging to the library

5. the tail of our cat

6. the happiness of the child

Speech marks (1)

We use **speech marks** to show that someone is talking. Speech marks are sometimes called **inverted commas**. The speech marks go around everything that is said, including its punctuation.

- "I like to watch television."

- Meena said, "My favourite programme is 'The News'."

Get started

Copy out these sentences, underlining the speech in each one. One has been done for you.

1. Mrs Handley said, "Today we will be busy."

2. She continued, "We have a lot of learning to do."

3. "Please will you read page twelve?" the teacher asked.

4. "Find three facts about Romans."

5. Mrs Handley told us, "Write down the information."

6. "I've found a great fact!" called Kyle.

7. Mrs Handley asked, "What is it?"

8. "Romans paid their soldiers in salt!"

Try these

Copy out each sentence. Then label it 'correct' or 'incorrect' to show whether or not it has the correct punctuation to show speech. One has been done for you.

1. "What did you" find out? asked Mrs Handley: *incorrect*

2. Lucas said, "I learnt that the Romans wore togas."

3. "Peyton added," I learnt that they built straight roads.

4. Meena said, Their armies were "strong".

5. "They liked to have baths!" said Harriet.

6. Mrs Handley said, "This is very good work!"

7. She continued, "Do you have any more facts for me"?

8. Kyle said, "I think they ate some strange things."

Now try these

Copy and complete these sentences by adding your own speech. The speech should be a complete sentence, with its punctuation.

1. While she was at the zoo, Millie said, "_____"

2. When she woke up, Mum said, "_____"

3. At the library, Kate said, "_____"

4. Whilst eating dinner, Tom said, "_____"

5. Schmidt said, "_____"

6. Talia asked, "_____"

Speech marks (2)

Remember, we use **speech marks** to show that someone is talking. The speech marks go around everything that is said, including its punctuation.

If a statement in speech comes after an explanation such as 'Bea said', the explanation ends with a comma.

- Bea said, "I'm going to play football."

- Mum said, "I'm going to play tennis."

Get started

Copy and complete these sentences, correcting the punctuation between the underlined words. One has been done for you.

1. Dad <u>said. "I'm</u> proud to have such a sporty family."

   Answer: *Dad said, "I'm proud to have such a sporty family."*

2. "Perhaps I'll go and play <u>squash! he</u> added.

3. Mum <u>replied, That</u> sounds like a good idea."

4. "Why don't you learn tennis with <u>me"? she</u> asked.

5. Bea <u>suggested "You</u> could come to football too."

6. Dad <u>sighed, Now I "don't</u> know what to do."

7. <u>Then "I said, I'm</u> going to stay here and play computer games."

8. <u>Dad "agreed That</u> sounds like the best plan to me!"

Try these

Copy and complete these sentences by adding speech marks correctly. One has been done for you.

1. Tamir said, Last night there was a great film on TV.

   Answer: *Tamir said, "Last night there was a great film on TV."*

2. Did you watch it? he asked Ria.

3. Do you mean the one about the pirates? questioned Ria.

4. Tamir replied, That's right.

5. Yes I saw that – it was amazing! answered Ria.

6. Tamir said, I think there's another one on tonight.

7. Would you like to come over and watch it together? Ria asked.

8. Tamir replied, Yes please – that'd be much more fun.

Now try these

Copy and complete each speech sentence. Pay close attention to how you punctuate the speech and any explanations you want to include.

1. After winning the swimming competition, Mae said…

2. As he put the pizza on the table, Dad said…

3. When she went to play hockey, Michelle said…

4. As soon as she got in from school, Hana asked…

5. Smiling at my friend, I asked…

6. Frowning at his brother, Buzz shouted…